The 7 COMPONENTS OF VISION

The Proven Formula To Extraordinary Success

EL-ROY R. COOK

MEMORABLE PUBLISHING

BE UNFORGETTABLE

CONTENTS

PRAISE FOR
THE 7 COMPONENTS OF VISION

Wow wow wow wow!!!!! So much perspective in these pages. The timing of reading this book is so perfect! I am currently a Medicine graduate and coming from a background such a Bonteheuwel, this book has just put everything into perspective. Funny how there are 7 components and I've just completed 7 years. I have found at least 3 key principles in each of the components of vision that I will cherish forever. I will definitely keep this book handy as I embark on my new journey as a doctor. I am going to be reminded of my dreams and keep perspective with vision. I am so proud of El-Roy for encapsulating this difficult topic so well.

Dr. Chanell L. Classen

MBChB(Stell)

Are you thirsty for success? Are you dissatisfied with your present status and sincerely desiring greatness? Do you have a passionate hunger to unlock the greatness within you?

Then search no further! El- Roy. R. Cook latest book, "The 7 Components of Vision " is the classic masterpiece that totally encapsulates the ultimate strategy that will take you to your glorious destination!

I've had the rare privilege of meeting with some highly successful people from all walks of life regardless of their gender, age or level of education. I have found out that the common denominator responsible for their outstanding success is vision!

The 7 Components of Vision in simple but mind blowing, insightful language, details the core factors of a Vision-focused life and accurately shows that your ability to imagine big is a clear sign that you are well on your way to the success and greatness you will profoundly enjoy.

Vision is no respecter of persons. Whether you are born great or poor, healthy or physically challenged, Vision is one of the most critical vehicles that will transport you to greatness.

This book, coming from the soul of my erudite scholar friend and companion, is super excellent and highly transformational and could not have arrived at a better time like this period in my life when I have giant goals to achieve. With this companion in my hand and God in me, I confidently announce to you, that I'm indomitably a celebrated success!

Stephen Robert Emezue

Author, Relationship Counselor, President: Love Seeker's Academy.

Excellence and passion are only a few words to describe this book! The 7 Components of Vision is A MUST READ!!! The moment I started reading I was immediately drawn to each word and each page! It was instant and magnetic. This book could not have come at a better time; I have completed my Bachelors in Psychology and I have yet to embark on my post-grad journey. This book has given me so much insight and has given me a new fire to pursue my dreams by using The 7 Components of Vision to make that vision a success! Thank you for your contribution El-Roy R. Cook. Your wisdom and take on this topic gave me a new drive, and it is valued and appreciated. You really have put together a remarkable piece that's life-changing!

Alezandri C. Groenewaldt

Psychologist

Motivation, focus, passion and thought provoking are amongst the few words that spring to mind whilst reading this book. You have a unique way of taking the practicalities of life that we all experience daily and turning them into words of reality that we can so easily and simply resonate with. To have taken in this literature at the beginning of the year could not have come at a better time. It has supported my mind-set with positivity, drive and enthusiasm to take the bull "2020" by the horns and make it a success. It was exactly what I needed. The moment your book is published, I will be sure to encourage those around me to get a copy and study this life-changing book.

Royston Clark

Head Service Delivery, Old Mutual Wealth Servicing

The 7 Components of Vision grasps a very thorough distinction between vision and dreams, but the perfect marriage of the two. I love how, though the two concepts are singular, they co-exist at the same time. Every year I take stock of where I was 365 days prior, and how much growth I've achieved. This time around I'm challenged to engage and apply my mind, thanks to author of The 7 Components of Vision that explores how intentionally multi-faceted the implementation of vision is. I've always perceived myself to be an out-of-the-box thinker. I'm going to stretch those boundaries even more now!

Roxanne Francis
Digital Editor at BRICS Journal

El-Roy R. Cook's latest book The 7 Components of Vision is a timeless book for anyone wanting to maximize their results and achieve their wildest dreams.

Wayne Van Rooyen
Award Winning Actor

Why do some people achieve so much more than others? Mr Cook's new book, The 7 Components of Vision is an inspiring and thought provoking book that looks at every one that has made an impact in their arena of expertise from software billionaires, talk show hosts, scientific geniuses and professional athletes. The book unfolds each pillar of the 7 components to a vision with the intent to let you honestly consider how far you are from your dream or how close you are to your desired success in life. The 7 Components of Vision highlights the truths to the questions so often asked about these individuals who epitomise success like: ''what does it take to succeed in this life?''. In this simple yet profound book, this question and many others, are answered and the dreams we desire are given a proven blueprint to finally achieve them.

Dell Mabunda

I highlighted so much of the book because it is full of profound truths and solid foundations for those wanting to build and design a life they love and enjoy. I found it extremely encouraging and also very practical. I can implement it immediately.

Having had the blessed privilege to work with El-Roy R. Cook I know that the words written in the book were not just googled and complied. He does not merely practice what he preaches but preaches what he practises and therefore is a great example that if you do as the book ascribes your life will transform and you will reach success.

Mbali Mahlangu
Founder Isabel Africa and Business Speaker

These 7 Components Vision in El-Roy R. Cook's new book with its sub-sections are several perfect renditions of life's perfect roleplay and execution in achieving extraordinary success. It is practical examples one can easily relate to while it also provokes you to adjust the necessary shortcomings in your personal life in order to achieve your ultimate dreams.

Andre Johnson

Kings Word Ministries, President and Founder

DEDICATION

To my precious son

Asher Shearon-Cook, you are my greatest joy and

the epitomy of a realized dream.

INTRODUCTION

UNDERSTANDING VISION

Growing up in a small backroom that was scarcely big enough to house the single car it was built for, raised by a single mom who would work extremely hard to ensure we had our daily needs met and sadly had to navigate an already difficult life dealing with the burden of being unemployed far too often.

Through the challenges of these circumstances, dreams for a better life, free from the daily struggles, free from the misfortunes, the labels, and the troubles I experienced early on in my childhood became my lifelong quest. And has taken me to blissful highs I am immensely grateful for and unfortunately disappointing lows of total financial collapse, losing close friends who abandoned me when I was at my lowest, dismally failing numerous times and wrestling with suicidal thoughts that hang over my life like a dark cloud.

Against the odds, I have succeeded and after years of questioning what really separates those who achieve their ultimate dreams and those who do not, I have discovered the primary key. The key that will unlock abundant wealth and best quality of life you most desire. The key is not lack of talent or your lack of resources but simply the lack of a compelling vision. In this book you will discover the unmatchable power of vision. This book is the culmination of over a decade spent studying the lives of the highly successful and applying their principles to reap similar results.

There are so many variations and explanations on what vision and dreams are that it's easy to get confused. Vision and dreams can also take on different connotations based on the context it's used in. For clarity allow me to start by defining both. The Oxford Dictionary defines the two as the following:

> **Vision**: n. *1 The ability to see. 2 The ability to think about the future with imagination or wisdom.*
>
> **Dream**: n. *A series of pictures or events in a sleeping person's mind; something greatly desired; something unreal or impossible. v. 1 Have a dream while asleep; have an ambition or desire.*

What these two definitions establish is that although these two terms have so many similarities, they are vastly different. Vision requires wisdom and forethought. Dreaming happens when sleeping or a goal that is desired when a person is consciously thinking. Success in all spheres requires both dreaming big and having a strong vision.

People who settle and live mediocre lives far beneath their peak performance and highest potential do so not because they have no dreams, but because they have no clear vision. Countless people dream; they see the end goal but hardly have any idea of the steps needed to be taken to realize those dreams. When you have a vision attached to your dream you discover the requirements, uncover the challenges and set clear boundaries you have to stay within to ensure the dream is realized.

Without a strong vision people will find themselves pursuing their dreams without a plan which increases their chances of failure because there are very few things of prestige, if any at all, that are achieved without a plan. A dream no matter how amazing it may be remains a wishful fantasy unless it's backed by a strong vision.

A dream can be compared to a game of darts with the centre of the dartboard as your ultimate dream. To ensure you hit the target will require total commitment, embracing failure and high focus. These are some of the components of vision working together to ensure you hit the target. If you lack vision no matter how lofty the goal or noble the ambition you will never hit the target.

What separates those who hit the target of their dreams from those who don't is not intellect, lack of money or talent even, but lack of vision. **That's why the poorest man alive is not the man without any money, but the man without a vision for his life.** Vision comprises of the strategic actions taken in response to your life's purpose. Vision is the roadmap to your destination and the blueprint to your dream.

Dreaming big will cost you nothing, but having a vision will cost you everything, and at times cause you to move beyond the threshold of some of your disappointments and fears. A blind man once asked God, "God can there be anything worse than losing my sight?" God replied "yes, having no vision." Sight is the function of the eyes, but vision is the application of the mind. It's the wisdom to move from where you are to where you are going. **That's why the most powerful force available to mankind is not eyesight but vision: mind-sight. Vision produces resourcefulness, creativity and innovation.**

In the Biblical story of Joseph, a Hebrew slave, who went from being a prisoner to becoming Prime Minster, he was not just a big dreamer but a great visionary. He was summoned from the prison to the palace to interpret the Egyptian Pharaoh's dream and the dream detailed how the Egyptian Nation would go through seven years where there was plenty of food to eat followed by seven years of harsh famine. To prepare for the seven years of famine and ensure they had enough food available Joseph did more than just interpreted Pharaoh's dream. He deployed a vision so effective that they became a source of provision for the entire then known world during the time of the famine. There are a lot of people who are good at articulating the problems that exist in society, but it's only visionary leaders like Joseph who tailor the solution.

What may have caused the Mcadonalds brothers to experience early success in their fast-food restaurant may have been their creativity and amazing entrepreneurial drive. But what took their restaurant to every corner of the world was the visionary leadership of Ray Kroc. **Vision will exploit the gift and produce extraordinary results.**

What built Apple into one of the leading multibillion dollar corporations was not just the engineering genius of Steve Wozniak, but the visionary leadership of Steve Jobs. Geniuses may produce innovation, but it's only visionaries that will drive it to its maximum potential.

THE 7 COMPONENTS OF VISION™

Why, you may ask should vision have components? Well, simply because components work in collaboration to achieve a common goal. It is when the components are correctly assembled that it results in a fully functioning system. For example, a car is a functional system that comprises of the wheels, the steering wheel, the engine, and many other parts. Similarly, in solving a puzzle, when the pieces are fitted together the picture should be exactly as it is on the box - that's your dream - with the different puzzle pieces being the components of vision. Each piece of the puzzle is necessary; each is needed to complete the puzzle, which is your dream.

In a similar manner, the 7 Components of Vision will work together for the realization of your dream. People who became highly successful from all walks of life will tell you that they can attribute their success to mastering either one or all of these components. It is the unwritten code that deligently guided to realize their aspirations and achieve heights others only dream of.

Mastering either one of the 7 Components of Vision makes you an asset and brings you one step closer to realizing your ultimate dreams. Master them all and you become a force to be reckoned with! I have experienced devastating consequences when violating many of the 7 Components of Vision, however, I have experienced extraordinary success when applying them. You will go through a similar process. Through the 7 Components of Vision you will finally discover why high levels of success is not a mystery for those who are certain about the outcome, but a science. This is not a quick roadmap to success, but a call to a lifetime commitment to its principles, a call to enjoy the journey in all its nuances and appreciate the success at every stage.

THINKING BIG

There is no nobility in modesty or thinking small.
Dream bigger dreams, set grander goals and there would be
absolutely no limits to how far you can go.

Everything you could ever see in the world, every great invention, every technological advancement and every tall skyscraper is a manifestation of thoughts, and if you can think it, know that it's possible. God will never give you a dream that you do not have the potential to fulfil, and sometimes the only reason why you are not there yet is because you simply have not discovered the requirements. One of the very first requirements is to think big. That's why thinking big is the first component of vision. Your life can only go as far as your thoughts. Big thoughts are the driving force behind the lives of all high achievers.

It is a widely held belief that thinking big requires more effort. This is the reason why many people limit the size of their dreams not because it is impossible, but because they believe they are incapable. There is however no greater effort required in thinking big than thinking small. If you are going to aim at anything you might as well ensure that the target is big enough to hit. Thinking small will limit the amount of success you are capable of achieving, thinking big will increase it exponentially.

Thinking big is not just wishful thinking but it engages the mind's cognitive and creative ability to shape the desires you want to see in your head first before it starts to manifest powerfully in reality. You have to have a vivid picture in your mind first before it can become tangible in your life. Thinking big will spur you on into prompt action and restless pursuit to uncover the requirements of what it takes to make your dreams possible. **That's why it doesn't matter where you are at now; a picture of your tomorrow will enable you to see beyond the obstacles, energize your spirit and give you a new hope to press on with more vigour.**

Out of all my accomplishments, my life-changing books and my transformational seminars, none of them were achieved with brilliant strategy or vast resources, but because I thought big in a small place. Thinking big allowed me to imagine the future I wanted for myself and filled me with the determination to work diligently towards it until the abstract became concrete. American business magnate Bill Gates did not pursue billions, he pursued the problems he was wired to solve. It gave him something bigger than himself to work towards. The reason why your dream needs to be significantly big is because you need to have something so compelling and greater than your current reality that it will cause you to push beyond your limits and overcome any odds.

BUILD STEP BY STEP

As valuable as thinking big is, what is equally important is that you learn to build step by step. Every great dream has a small start and every step you take towards that dream becomes the platform that will take you higher. The IPhone 11 is the evolution of producing the 1st one. Each latest model built on both the successes and failures of the previous one in order to improve. If you wait to be perfect to start you engage in a futile exercise called paralysis by over-analysis. In the success equation perfection is not always the main goal; progress is.

Highly successful Film Producer Tyler Perry's first audience was a meagre 30 people in the early years of his career, in which he experienced tremendous loss and even became homeless. You have to be faithful with the few before you can earn the respect of the multitudes. You have to master one level well before you are afforded the opportunity to go to the next. And don't become discouraged when the rewards don't always match your effort. Sometimes what others might perceive as failure might just be part of your process. Just like Tyler Perry, you might not get it on the first, second or even on several attempts, but **one day the many steps you took towards your dream will all add up, and the next step you take will be the move that changes everything.**

Building step by step is also about learning to finish the small things first. Finishing the small things helps you develop an instant sense of victory and gives you a positive mind-set to attempt even bigger tasks. Before you can do more or scale your business, master one level. When you do that you will start asking yourself questions like, "How can we grow this, do more or take this further?" The performance is what will determine the progress. Coca Cola has been in existence for 134 years and when it started out in 1886 it only sold a meagre 9 drinks per day. Today they are consumed at an astonishing rate of more than 1.9 billion drinks per day. **You only get to push the limits once you have mastered where you are. The road towards your dreams is a step by step process, not a miracle.**

Think about where you would like to be in the next 5 to 10 years from now, what steps you are willing to take, and what sacrifices you are willing to make to ensure your dream doesn't just become another unrealized fantasy?

> *Thinking big must encompass a purpose that is clear, a passion that is genuine and plans that must be executed.*

PURPOSE THAT IS CLEAR

You must think big dreams to the extent that it furthers your purpose. People who fail regularly are often doing something unrelated to their purpose. If you don't know your purpose you will never discover what you're truly passionate about, nor establish the strategic partnerships that are essential to fulfil your dream. Purpose precedes partnerships, products and plans. Planning is the product of being purposely driven. Purpose ensures plans are laid out, the parameters are clear and the provision is available.

No matter who you are or where you are born, there is a purpose that made your existence necessary. Purpose is more valuable than power. Powerful people without purpose is like a ship without a rudder. It has nothing to direct it. Purpose is more important than income. Income is the reward for adding value, but purpose is the fulfilment of your life's calling. No one can really teach you your purpose. They can help you identify it, but purpose is a personal discovery of what you are born to do. **An airplane not in flight will rapidly decrease its lifespan because it's not fully living out the reason behind its design. Anything not directed towards its purpose dies a premature death.** Sadly, there are too many people who have died without having ever truly lived because they didn't live out their purpose.

There is an area in your life where you are profoundly gifted and serving it to the world is the key to a fulfilled life and will lead you to a wealthy place. How does one discover their purpose you might ask? **What excites you? What burdens are you overwhelmed with to lift? What gifts have you been blessed with to serve? And what problems are you wired for to solve?** For Bill Gates it was computer software, for Nelson Mandela it was the struggle for liberation.

There is a reason why certain things bother you and certain things don't mean much to you, not because they are not important but because what makes you come alive is the area that defines your purpose for being. An airplane is manufactured in such a way to enable it to fly. Your purpose reveals the reason behind your design.

People that know their purpose don't waste their time on petty things. They focus their time and energy on the things that brings them closer to realizing their goals. When you are in your purpose you will have peace because you are doing what makes you come alive. When you are in your purpose you don't look for external validation. Your validation comes from living in alignment with that cause. When you start living purposefully some doors will automatically open and the whole universe starts to conspire to assist you with realizing those desires because it recognizes a man and woman who have stepped into their purpose.

Understanding the reason behind why you desire a certain goal is very crucial for success. Your purpose is your why; it's the fuel that will drive you and the fire burning deep down in your soul. Thriving organizations and highly successful people are what they are because they are driven by people with a strong why. Celebrated liberation icon Nelson Mandela was willing to be imprisoned for his whole life and even die in order to bring liberation to his people because of his why. When your why is bigger than you, you will be willing to endure any hardship and discomfort to realize that dream.

Everything you do in life must speak to your why. My why is to live a life free from the abject poverty and troubled childhood I experienced being raised by a single parent, in a small background. And to provide a good quality of life for my family and impact the world with my gifts. What is your why? Unless you establish your clear 'why' you won't be driven to reach for your dream hard enough.

When you know your 'why' it solidifies your focus. When you know your 'why' the difficult choices become easy. When you know your 'why' it becomes a compelling force that drives you forward. **That's why it is not about how difficult your circumstances but about how strong your why.** Never pursue any goal without knowing your why because your why is what will sustain the fire and keep you going when faced with failure.

PASSION THAT IS GENUINE

Purpose is the source of why you do what you do, planning is your strategy, but passion is the spirit in which you do it. True satisfaction comes when what you do is part of your life's purpose and this is nothing short of what you're passionate about. Passionate people are excited and are the most alive because they doing what they genuinely love. Purpose that lacks passion often results in minimal success. Only the ones filled with passion for what they do are driven to produce beyond what is expected. The skilled worker doesn't always get rewarded highly in life but the passionate one does.

What causes people to deliver dazzling plays and magical performances is when they are imbued with passion. Passionate people remain excited about the dream long after the initial hype has passed. Don't commit yourself to things you don't have the passion to complete. The currency of vision is passion, and the fuel of perseverance is passion. **Passion will get you staying the course when the stakes are high. Nothing else will stand the test of time except passion**.

Sadly, passion is a dying trait. But without passion people soon lose the drive for what they aim to accomplish. Focus may expel distractions and perseverance may give you courage in times of trouble, while self-discipline may help you put on the right behaviour, but passion will give you an intrinsic motivation to keep on going. Passion helps you develop unconditional love for what you do. Great accomplishments are not always outworked by geniuses, but those who remain passionate about their dream.

PLANS THAT ARE EXECUTED

Dreaming big must translate into plans that are executed. Your plan is your blueprint, your guiding manual. Planning becomes the benchmark on which proper decisions are made. Planning causes you to place higher priority on the goal, respect the time allocated and manage resources wisely. **Planning separates the wishful thinker from the strategic doer. Planning brings logical conclusions to your dreams before you begin.**

In this world of time constrained realms, every second counts. Planning therefore becomes the seed that minimizes error and maximizes the time frame of your life. Wars are not won by simply rushing into battle but by carefully plotted plans. Writing down your plans helps kick start the process of clarification. A plan that is written down can be worked on, adjusted and most importantly, executed.

Most of our time is spent planning our lives to the finest detail, and playing our dreams out until it becomes reality. Some of us, however, have become experts in planning that it has resulted into a full time day dreaming job that never moves outside our head. We plan all these elaborate things in our head, we become the heroes in our own epic story, reliving the sensation of victory only in our heads, yet we fail to put our plan into action.

No matter how great and colourful a dream may seem, it can only be realized if you take action. That's why a business plan is not a prerequisite to starting a business, action is. I didn't have grand plans when I wrote my first book, I just did it. Planning that doesn't lead to action is a futile exercise of the mind. **If good things happen to those who wait, then great things happen to those who diligently plan and take action.**

Planning is not just about how well you plan, but more importantly about how well you execute the plan. You can plan the best diet and study the most effective techniques to get into tip top shape, but if you never get into the gym and commit yourself to the process you will never achieve your health goal.

There's a time to dream and there's a time to arise and take action. It doesn't matter how trivial a dream may seem, the important thing is to start doing something about it. A vision is meant to be run. What is important is to take the first action step, and while you're at it, the dream slowly translates into reality.

7 POWERFUL BENEFITS OF PLANNING

1. *Your plan is forward thinking.*

2. *Planning gives you a strategic order to follow through on your goals.*

3. *It establishes the resources you need to achieve the goal.*

4. *Challenges and red-flags are highlighted.*

5. *Timeline for completion of the goal is set in motion.*

6. *Your priorities are clearly defined.*

7. *It holds you accountable to a predetermined course.*

CHANGE YOUR EXPOSURE

In order to think outrageously big you need to change what you are exposed to in order to lift the perception of what you think is possible. What books are you reading at the moment, what environments are you frequently exposed to and what people do you regularly hang around with? These places will either nourish and reinforce your commitment to your dream or reduce it until it no longer becomes that compelling. One of the common reasons many successful people attained extraordinary heights is because what they were exposed to dramatically changed. They were exposed to places and people that enriched their lives and stretched their thinking.

Go to the places and hang around the people that will provoke the greatness in you. You cannot begin to change your experience until you do what you regularly exposed to. Changing your exposure fosters a new belief in you of what is really possible. In today's world average has become such a big epidemic, however, when you are exposed to great things you are inspired to do your greatest work.

HAVE THE RIGHT ATTITUDE

Big thinkers rarely have a bad attitude. Their desire to achieve more is what puts them in a positive mental state. Studies have proven that 85% of the reason why people get promoted and progress further in life is because of their attitude, and only 15% is because of their knowledge or job experience. The studies are unanimous; the right attitude is a critical factor to achieve highly in life. You want to be the owner of a multi-million dollar corporation but you are skeptical in your ability to achieve that goal. You then think you can't do it and come up with multi-million dollar excuses why you can't. Have faith and speak those things you want to see into being, and believe it with the attitude that it has already been done.

The famous Italian Explorer Christopher Columbus had an obscure background and came from no nobility. Having greater ambitions than being a mere ship merchant he decided that he would go on the most ambitious voyage to travel the ocean and discover new lands. Although he had neither the skill nor experience, he lobbied influential people for several years and even insisted being called by a new title, 'Lord of The Seas' for this bold undertaking. His persistence eventually paid off and the Catholic Monarchs of Spain agreed to sponsor his first journey.

What happened? His belief in himself fostered the habits and the attitudes that drove him in the direction of those thoughts. Your life will move in the direction of your most dominant thoughts, and people will respond to you and treat you exactly how you see yourself. It is within your power to set your own price and demand which you deem worthy.

THINKING BIG MAKES YOU FEARLESS

Those who don't think big lack the self-confidence and self-belief that is necessary to thrust them forward into greater achievements. To go for uncommon and outrageously large goals takes a fearless spirit that small thinkers do not possess.

Thinking small leads to un-inspiring, less exciting and mediocre goals; the irony is that the competition for smaller goals is compellingly greater than bigger ones. Think for example the ratio of people pursuing their PHD's compared to those who just stop at one degree, or the few people daring to risk it all pursuing their ultimate dreams while countless people go to a job daily that they do not find fulfilment in. And as bestselling author Timothy Ferris points out in his book *The Four Hour Work Week, it is easier to raise $1 000, 000 than it is $100 00.* In a world where everyone's settling for far less than what they have the potential to achieve, your best chances of making it is to set insanely big goals and actually go for them. It might scare you at first, but focus on your dreams instead of your fears and it might just surprise you how real they become.

Those who are fearless walk away from any relationship that no longer values them, don't accept roles that are far beneath them, don't allow the opinions of others to discourage them, nor allow their circumstances to cause them to redefine their goals, and choose to travel down uncertain roads that profoundly challenges them.

START WITH THE END IN MIND

You might fail but that's not the sum of who you are. Never allow moments that have not gone as planned to define you or the premature conclusions of others to become the boundary of how far you can reach. If you fill your mind with rich thoughts you become the antidote to your problems, and if you think as big as you possibly can you place a demand on a higher self for you to grow into. What matters most in life is not what others think of you but the stories you continually tell yourself. You need to become your own cheerleader first in order to become the champion you know you are.

What you tell yourself daily can either become self-fulfilling prophecies of doom or be the seeds that become the catalyst for greater things. Those who think big always have the end in mind at their forefront. That's why it's important to always start with the end in mind. It won't always make things easier, but it will give you courage in times of setbacks, and hope to carry on no matter how numerous the failures or difficult the circumstances.

When highly successful comedian Steve Harvey was discouraged by one of his teachers from writing his dream of being on TV one day, his father enthusiastically encouraged him to write his dream on a piece of paper and read it out loud to himself every morning when he got out of bed, and in the evening before he went to back to sleep. In other words, have the end of the goal at your forefront constantly. Years later that dream became more than a reality with him now being on TV 7 days a week and a bestselling author. **When you write your dreams down you are starting with the end in mind and making a personal declaration to yourself that you are certain about the outcome you want to achieve and will not stop until it has fully manifested.**

Make up vision boards and affirmation notes and put them in the places that you frequent; whether it's your refrigerator at home, your car or office in your workplace. They will help hold you accountable and serve as daily reminders of the goals you have set out to achieve. Your dreams are not too big or too irrational; if you can visualize and write it down in due course it will eventually come to pass just like Steve Harvey's dreams did. Start with the end in mind, think big.

BENEFITS OF THINKING BIG

- ✓ *Thinking big challenges you to perform at your highest level. All Olympic super athletes are essentially big thinkers first.*

- ✓ *Thinking big gives you a better picture of your tomorrow.*

- ✓ *Thinking big allows you to be in a positive state. You cannot think big and be negative at the same time.*

- ✓ *Thinking big gives you a sense of mission and purpose.*

- ✓ *Thinking big challenges you and stretches your mind. A stretched mind is an engaged mind, and an engaged mind is in a peak state for optimal performance.*

- ✓ *If you think small you will do little, but if you think big that's what you will become.*

- ✓ *Thinking big allows you to operate out of your imagination not your limitations and causes you to push beyond the boundaries not accept them. People that live poor lives are living out of their limitations not their imagination and that's why they settle.*

- ✓ *Thinking big is a powerful motivator and the catalyst to an extraordinary life.*

- ✓ *Nothing limits achieving like small thinking; nothing expands possibilities like big thinking. You are what you limit yourself to be.*

- ✓ *Thinking big places a higher demand on you to be more than what you are right now. It's impossible to truly think big and remain the same.*

A HEALTHY SELF-IMAGE

*Your self-image is the number one quality that
will lead to extraordinary success.*

The second Component of Vision is having A Healthy Self-Image. The most powerful and fundamental change that can occur in any individual's life is a paradigm shift. It's a change in the way they see themselves; their self-image. Your self-image can change your health, your wealth and the quality of your relationships. No change is more permanent and no change is more profound.

The most common way to determine your self-image is to take a look at your results. Your self-image will determine the places you go to, the people you hang out with and what you prioritize. Everything about you says something about you. Where you live, the position you hold at work and the people you associate yourself with.

What denies people from their best and living the extraordinary life they were designed to have is their self-image. The real obstacles are not outside, the real obstacles people are faced with daily is themselves. Before you can change your circumstances, there must be a change in your paradigm - a paradigm shift, a change in the way you see yourself.

A paradigm shift also represents a departure in a conventional way of thinking, a breakthrough. Mobile Phones, and innovative apps like Facebook and Uber are all some of the technology that took us forward into the future and forever changed how we perform certain functions. Paradigm shifts that are positive move things forward and make it better. If the paradigm doesn't change the behaviour will persist and the results stays the same.

Circumstances change for the good or the bad because you are the catalyst influencing that change. You are not doing in order to become, but you are becoming, and therefore you do. How people are programmed is so powerful that the intrinsic nature of a person will always override their basic needs.

Your self-image is not the image reflecting back at you in the mirror, but the image you hold about yourself within your mind. Your self-image is one of the most dominating forces ruling your life. The way you see yourself dictates to every decision you make, forms the foundation of your reality, impacts every area of your life, determines the quality of your living and is constantly on display for everyone else to see. **If you see yourself as defeated then you already are before you've even began.**

One of the greatest mistakes people make is trying to change something on the outside without making the necessary changes from within. Who you are might be the greatest obstacle standing in the way of the health, wealth and quality relationships you want.

Man's most dominant need is not their need for security, significance or survival but it is the need to remain consistent with how they see themselves. Many people have upgraded their homes and cars, but certain behaviours continue to persist like a bad attitude and recklessness because the expression is in line with their self-image.

That's why the key to your paradigm shift is a mind transformation and not just motivation. I am sure you can think of someone right now in your life that's forever highly motivated but has not moved substantially forward in their personal life. **Not that motivation is bad, but motivation without application is just emotional intoxication.** Motivation is emotional, transformation is psychological. Motivation is temporal, transformation is perpetual. Motivation is about doing, transformation is about being. In other words, who do I have to be in order to step into the life I truly want?

Transformation deals with those key ingredients that profoundly affect who we become and how we engage the world. That's why, a 'To Do List' is transactional but a 'Not

To Do' list is transformational. There are certain things that you have to learn to stop doing now in your life that could dramatically change the trajectory of your destiny. In my life I have learned to stop doing several things.

I have stopping checking up on those who have consistently proven that they don't have time for me.

I have stopped wasting my time, energy and resources on the things that do not support the causes I represent.

I have stopped entertaining other people's drama or engaging in pointless arguments.

I have stopped allowing those with no good fruit to have a voice in my life.

I have stopped looking at who doesn't support me and started appreciating the few people who do.

I have stopped going to places or hanging around people who make me feel inadequate and diminish my worth.

I have stopped trying to be everybody's hero and worked on saving myself first.

I have stopped looking at whether the grass is greener on the other side and started to fertilize where I am.

I have stopped looking for money and have started working on becoming a person of value.

I have stopped allowing minor things to distract me, and focused my energy entirely on the major things that enrich me.

Sometimes before the start of, 'The Best of You' is a 'Stop To Do'. Maybe there are a few things you should stop doing today that you are aware that if you could just have the courage to stop you will gain the strength to grow.

Before you can become a better person and an exemplary role model, you need to take inventory of who you are. At the core of leadership is self-leadership. You must lead yourself well first before you can gain the privilege to eventually lead others.

EMBRACE CHANGE

A dog was crying all day and the neighbour asked the owner "but why is the dog crying so much?" The owner replied, "because his laying on a nail" The neighbour then asked, "why doesn't he just move" the owner then finally said "because it's not hurting badly enough."

Sadly, countless people are just like that dog; in toxic relationships, disadvantaged circumstances and comfortable with the pain and drama because it's just not hurting badly enough. And often it will require a traumatic experience like the loss of a loved one, being fired from their job or going through a painful breakup that becomes the catalyst for a paradigm shift.

You will never recognize the urgency of changing until you've beaten your wife too far and she leaves you for another man that finally treats her like the queen she is. You will never recognize the urgency of changing until that drink has caused you to crash into another car and left you paralyzed from the waist down. You will never recognize the urgency of changing until you lose that job and start to realize its true value. Don't wait for turbulent times to come before you make significant changes for your growth. Totally embrace the changes that are beneficial to your goals. I guarantee you, it will be worth it.

BELIEVE YOU CAN!

In 1999 Jack Ma, founder of The Alibaba Group, a billion-dollar internet business, said to his team that they would IPO in 2002, however, it only happened in 2014, 12 years later. The first time the Time Magazine covered him they said he was crazy. Although he miscalculated the timing of his outstanding success, what is important is that he believed he could and eventually did.

When life hands you a curve ball and things go terribly wrong, what will keep you going is not just positive thinking or will power but the self-image you hold. Your self-image will help you stay positive amidst numerous disappointments and give you the assurance that no matter how devastating the failure, if you keep on going you will eventually get to where you want to go. And like billionaire Jack Ma, you may not always achieve your dreams in the timeframe you have set out, but if you persevere, you will eventually get there.

When I started out writing I couldn't spell well, had poor school grades and I had barely made it through high school. I was honestly the last person you would ever think would write a book one day. Several books later, having published multiple books of other people and even ghost wrote some, what happened? I believed I could and that's why I did.

What am I saying to you today? Don't lower the expectations of yourself - increase the effort and remove the limitations. It's not who you think you are that holds you back, it's who you think you are not. I know you might be saying, "but what if I can't?" I would like to encourage you and say, but what if you can? "What if I fail again?" – But what if you fly? Those who regularly win big in life have mastered the second component of vision, which is having a healthy self-image. They believe they can and that's why they do. **When things don't always work out for you, perhaps change the strategy, but never redefine your dream because of your circumstances.**

COMMON EXCUSES PEOPLE TELL THEMSELVES

I AM TOO OLD OR TOO YOUNG

After spending almost 27 years in prison Nelson Mandela only became president of South Africa at the age of 77. Susan Boyle went on to have UK's bestselling album of all time after her famous appearance on Britain's Got talent. She only found success at the age of 47. And the King of Pop, Michael

Jackson, started his music career at the tender age of 13. They all eliminate the idea that you are never too old or too young to start.

I AM NOT SMART ENOUGH

Hollywood famous actor Drew Barrymore was a school dropout at just age 13 and billionaire Richard Branson has dyslexia. Both of them are highly successful and prove that your 'I Can!' is more important than your IQ.

LACK OF RESOURCES

Oscar Winner Halle Berry stayed in a homeless shelter in her early 20s and multiple Ballon d'or award winner Cristiano Ronaldo grew up in a tin roofed house. What stops most people from reaching their ultimate dreams is rarely their lack of resources or the difficulty of their circumstances but their abundance of excuses.

DISABILITY

Grammy Award winner Stevie Wonder is blind and world-celebrated motivational speaker and bestselling author Nick Vujicic has no arms or legs. They both are unquestionable proof that it's not disability but mentality that holds most people captive.

BLAME

People who always blame others for their circumstances are full of lies. Leaders take ownership for both their successes and their failures. Those who succeed in life look for others to thank for the success they so graciously enjoy. Those who don't always look for alibis to blame for their failure.

In all the above-mentioned cases one thing that becomes compellingly clear is that people who always give alibis for their lack of success, there will always find the exception. Moreover, when people look for external sources to appoint blame for their lack of success they avoid taking responsibility, miss the opportunity to learn the lesson and fail to grow from it.

BE YOUR OWN HERO

One of the young men I am mentoring once told me he was going through a really hard time where he was living. He proposed that moving somewhere else might change things in which I simply replied, "change in location doesn't always guarantee change in direction, new decisions do". Your job is not the reason you are unhappy; you are. Happiness is a personal decision and when you decide to be happy you will be. It's not your wife's job to make you a man; you are one, step up. **Don't determine your value or identity based on external factors. A lion does not roar to prove he's a lion, he is a lion therefore he roars.**

A Wiseman was once asked by a Youngster who had a bird in his hand whether the bird was alive or dead. The Youngster knew that if the Wiseman said the bird is alive he would just increase his grip and suffocate the bird to death and if the Wiseman said the bird is dead he would just open his hand and set it free and it would fly away. The Wiseman having the foresight of what the Youngster would do simply responded, "the answer is in your hands."

Where you are now in your life is no mere coincidence but a direct reflection of who you are and the sum of your decisions. Like the Wiseman told the Youngster that day, I would like to remind you today that the answer is in your hands. Nobody is coming to rescue you - be your own hero.

ROAR!!!

There was a day a long time ago when a little lion cub was born and there was a brutal attack on the pride of lions. The lion cub's mother and the father in trying to save him threw him into the bushes. Sadly, the mother and father lion was massacred. After the massacre the lion cub woke up all alone. Nothing even to remember his parents by, all he knew was that he was alone, barely functioning at an early age.

Subsequently sheep came by making sounds, "baa baa, baa baa" and the little lion cub came out. One of the sheep came up and rubbed up against him, "baa baa, baa baa". And before you knew it within a few months the lion cub was one of the crew, making the same sounds, "baa baa, baa baa...". One day a pride of lions came and killed all the sheep amongst them and now the little lion cub was a big lion going, "baa baa, baa baa". He was horrified by it all and shocked. One giant lion came over to him and smacked him on the head saying, "what the hell is wrong with you?!" The lion took him by the head to a puddle of water. He looked at his reflection in the puddle and saw that he was not a sheep, but he remained unconvinced. The lion then proceeded to feed him some of the sheep, however, he tried to spit it out because his was a vegetarian you know.

He was horrified and couldn't eat his brethren, however, the big lion stuffed it down his throat and something magical happened inside. He finally remembered who he was. There is something inside of you that nothing can take away, something so powerful that it can be kind and strong. As the food went down a crazy thing happened - He stopped saying baa baa and he roared.

Your self-image will determine your self-belief and your self-belief will either give you wings to soar or form mental prisons that hold you back. Your self-belief will make you see yourself small or big in the estimation of others and all you do. A lion with a sheepish belief system can never live out its lion potential. Be the roaring lion that awakens to his full potential. The day you discover the truth about who you are, just like the lion did that day, you will let go of past perceived limitations and roar.

96% of businesses fail within the first ten years. But you will be the exception; roar!

A lion is not the biggest or the fastest animal in the jungle but it's king of the jungle because of its attitude; roar!

A lion doesn't demand respect, it commands it; roar.

When the walls seem to be caving in your life; roar.

For every closed door, missed opportunity and 'no' you are going to prove them wrong; roar.

The scales will tip in your favour, and when you roar, that's the unique sound of the warrior you are; roar.

BENEFITS OF HAVING A HEALTHY SELF-IMAGE

GIVES YOU AN UNPARALLELED ADVANTAGE

With a healthy self-image you are certain of who you are and can progress quicker. Because the clarity of whom you are gives you unlimited power and an unparalleled advantage.

CAUSES YOU TO CELEBRATE OTHERS

With a healthy self-image you are mature enough to celebrate those around you without feeling threatened or intimidated by their success. When you celebrate others' success the action will be reciprocated when you achieve success because the harvest you reap is always a representation of the seed you've sown.

CLARIFIES YOUR OBJECTIVES

With a healthy self-image you will have clarity about your objectives, and it's that clarity that will increase your productivity and help you remain focused.

PRIORITIZES WHAT'S IMPORTANT

With a healthy self-image you minimize the time on things that add little or no value to your dreams and choose to fully prioritize those activities essential to achieving your goals.

THEY WORK ON THEMSELVES

With a healthy self-image you work harder on improving yourself than anything else. It's much easier to work on yourself than on programs and people. You are the number one catalyst to the extraordinary life you want.

FILLS YOU WITH SUPERNATURAL CONFIDENCE

People with a healthy self-image are certain of who you are and don't wait for others to tell them who they are. Fulfilling their life's work is what fills them with supernatural confidence and validation.

3RD COMPONENT:

TOTAL COMMITMENT

The uncommitted life is a life of half-hearted effort, mediocre performance and poor results.

One of life's greatest ironies is that there are countless highly talented people who have not attained any substantial success, not because they can't but because they fail to live by the 3rd Component of Vision, Total Commitment.

Everyone who dreams must hold themselves responsible for realizing that dream. If you have a big dream in your mind, then you can also bring it to life - There is, however, a lot of effort involved. Without total commitment progress is a far-fetched phenomenon.

But what is Total Commitment really? Total commitment is the farmer planting a seed and watering it daily. It's the champion super athlete practicing for hours and hours each day. It's the Grammy Award winning artist, the innovator and the people who do what everyone else thought was impossible. Thomas Edison, the man who is credited for inventing the light bulb said he knows 999 ways how not to make a light bulb, because he failed that many times before successfully making a functional light bulb. Talk about determination, talk about unwavering commitment to a cause. This guy actually failed 999 times and still didn't quit, and finally on the 1000th attempt he succeeded. Today he is known throughout the world mainly due to his light bulb invention.

> *Failure is the decision to resign oneself to the unfavourable outcome of your pursuit; success is the committed decision to move beyond failure no matter how numerous.*

What people commit to is their choice and the effects of these choices can be seen in their lives. Think about mobile companies like Apple and Samsung. The reason they are leading in their industry of choice is because of their commitment to provide world-class mobile phones. Then there are companies like KFC and McDonalds, both of which serve fast food, yet none of the meals tastes like the other. Each company has their original recipe and is committed to preserving it. You don't become number one by chance but by hard work, determination and total commitment. These companies, and many others like them are undoubtedly proof of that.

The reason why undisputed 50-0 World Champion Boxer, Floyd Mayweather, and holder of the most Grand Slam tennis titles Serena Williams are consistently ranked number one is because they set ridiculously high standards that's hard to achieve for anyone that is not willing to put in the work. **Similarly in your own life, if the results are going to be uncommon the effort needs to be extraordinary.**

Every great dream you have in your heart comes at a price. No one stumbles upon massive success; it's the reward of consistent and diligent action. Once you put in the work you can expect the results. **Success is a deliberate attempt to an end goal and not an unexpected event, and although you might fail from time to time, it is by striving, that you are already winning.**

Countless people say they are committed to realizing their dreams until they discover the requirements, and then you realize they are really not that committed. It will cost you something to achieve your ultimate dreams, it will cost you something to improve the quality of your life and it will cost you something to go to the next level. Nothing worth having comes easy and if you are not willing to pay the price then you are not ready to reap the rewards of extraordinary success. Dreaming is easy but the implementation of the dream comes at a high cost and you first pay with total commitment.

WHAT IS THE MEASURE OF YOUR COMMITMENT?

I just love ballet dancers. Have you ever seen how they move; graceful, elegant and enchantingly magical? They move effortlessly with such perfect precision and exceptional coordination you would swear it was easy. That's until you try to do it yourself and discover that it's not as easy as it seems.

Often people perform brilliantly and make it look so easy, and you might be tempted to think you can master in a moment what they have actually practiced their entire lifetime to master and walk away feeling frustrated and disappointed when you do not immediately reap similar rewards. Before you can reap their results first match their effort, match their dedication, match their sacrifice and match their total commitment.

YOU CANNOT EXPECT ABOVE AVERAGE RESULTS WITH MEDIOCRE EFFORT

When it comes to pursuing your dream, nobody should be more determined, nobody should be more on fire, nobody should be more sold out and nobody should be more committed than you. What's the measure of your commitment? **What separates the greats from the ordinary is the measure of their commitment. The measure of commitment you give to your dream will determine the size of your rewards.**

How bad do you really want your dream? Your dream must become a compelling obsession that you relentlessly pursue and is constantly at the forefront of your life. It must be something you would gladly give up your time, sleep and comfort for, and if necessary endure the pain of failing, being misunderstood or looked at foolishly for a season in order to live in permanent victory one day.

BE CONSISTENT

Popularity is a fading phenomenon, but greatness is an enduring quality. Greatness requires consistency. Anybody can be great in a moment but to be great over time requires consistency. Great companies do not pop up overnight but they are built over a consistent period of time. One of the key traits to any great person rising is their consistency. That's why the ultimate test of your leadership is not just about how well you are performing now but whether or not you will be around 5-10 years from now sustaining the momentum and with your character still intact.

Being consistent is about rather starting slow and finishing hard than starting hard and finishing last. It's better to under promise and over deliver than to over promise and not measure up. It's better to show people your results than to share all your dreams and not realize them.

Consistency is also about having the resilience to continue in something when you encounter an obstacle and failure because there are vast challenges that you are going to encounter along the way that could discourage you from pursuing your dreams.

If you hit a tall oak tree with a sharp axe will it come down? Probably not, but if you continue on the same spot for a sustained period the tree will eventually come down no matter how tall the tree or deep its roots. And that's the true essence of consistency; it's not what you do once that gives you outstanding results, but the combination of your repeated effort. Every action you take is one step closer to your dream. Sadly, many people have not achieved their ultimate dreams because they too often grew despondent by the early results and gave up prematurely.

COMMIT TO GOOD VALUES

Commit yourself to values that do not compromise your success and maintain a good work ethic that will make you thrive no matter the circumstances.

What will ensure your success stands the test of time and possibly outlive you is the values that you have lived by and not just what you have accomplished. That's why a good character is more important than a big bank balance. A good character ensures that you have a strong moral compass, gains you respect amongst your peers and makes you a person that can easily be trusted. The reason why companies like

Microsoft continue to maintain their dominance is because of their commitment to not compromise their values and the integrity of their products. The value of integrity, honesty and respect for others are not often talked about in relation to the equation of success, and although there are certainly many who have achieved high levels of success without them it's only the truly great that makes it an indispensable part of their success.

Look at the sad fall of American beloved actor and Hollywood icon Bill Cosby who was found guilty of several sexual assault charges. Whether the allegations which were made against him were true or not, the fact was that he was a married man, and by committing adultery with so many women he brought his character into serious question, and by so doing sealed his fate. When you have a bad character you can lose the privileges your talent allows you to have and drastically diminish the size of your impact.

Values cannot be taught, it must be modelled. If you want those whom you lead to come early, you must come early. If you want to be respected, respect others. Treat people with the same dignity and respect you would demand from them. True success is not just in how highly talented you are but in the values you live by and the strength of your impact. Mother Theresa didn't have to have an impressive title nor was she extremely rich but she had a global impact. What are the values you are committed to? The wrong values can easily short-circuit your success but the right values allow you to have an enduring impact.

SELFLESS LEADERSHIP

Equally as important as good values is being committed to a great work ethic and being a selfless leader. What I like even more than the visionary leadership of the Biblical dreamer Joseph is his incredible work ethic and selfless leadership. When he was betrayed and sold into slavery by his own brothers, eventually landing up in Potiphar's house who was the captain of the palace guard, instead of moaning about his unfortunate circumstances Joseph served so well that he was promoted and became the Chief Butler. When he experienced another setback, and landed in prison due to being falsely accused, he continued to be a diligent worker and even there got placed in charge over all the other prisoners.

Part of the reason the Egyptian ruler Pharaoh heard about Joseph was because one of the prisoners that was with Joseph was eventually released and told Pharaoh about how Joseph had selflessly helped him in prison. Joseph's breakthrough came from an unlikely source. That's why you should never determine your performance based on who you serve.

Joseph knew that it was more important to add value to people by serving them than to be selfish and self-seeking. The results of his selfless leadership eventually paid off tremendous rewards for him. The best leaders are not just those who ascend to lofty positions by might or talent, but those who selflessly add value to others. To be a great leader like Joseph you must be willing to make things better for the people who follow you and help them to become the best versions of themselves.

Who would have thought that the prisoner who Joseph helped would one day recommend him to the Egyptian ruler Pharaoh? **Joseph teaches us a timeless lesson that is that the person that you might perceive below you might one day be in a position to significantly help you.** Value and appreciate everyone. Everyone is important. When you only form relationships with those who you perceive as valuable or are in a position to help you, you compromise your integrity and set yourself up for failure in the long run.

MANAGE THE LITTLE THINGS WELL

Many like to be complacent and blame their circumstances for their poor work ethic. They mistakenly assume that they will work harder or be better one day when their circumstances are more favourable. No wonder they are always overworked, underpaid and get passed over for promotion repeatedly. **The measure in which you manage the little things will determine the measure you receive in bigger things. Every harvest the farmer reaps is determined on the seeds he sows.**

The work you produce is a personal reflection of your deepest values, highest ideals and standard you hold yourself accountable to. A poor work ethic is a deterrent to greatness and will seep into all other areas of your life. Everything is connected. That's why you should strive to have a great work ethic just like Joseph and **set the bar so high that you become the standard that everyone else measures themselves up against.** What distinguished Joseph was that his work ethic was never based on his circumstances but his convictions. If you have a great work ethic you will be respected by your peers and superiors. If you have a great work ethic people might be smarter or more talented than you but if you can outwork them you will always be ahead of them.

Just as important as having a great work ethic, is working hard on your own personal dream. Don't just work hard on someone else's dream that you fail to fertilize your own garden. If you are domestic worker and your goal is to become a teacher one day, you can be the best domestic worker but if you don't work equally as hard on taking the necessary steps towards realizing that dream, within 5 years from now you will be nowhere closer to realizing that goal.

START TODAY

It's not our circumstances or failures that determine the course of our life but our decisions. Those who win big in life make a deliberate decision to do so.

They decide that they must win and that quitting is no longer an option. That despite everything they say to themselves, "I'm not going to stop until I win big!" They make up their mind to persevere and reach for their dreams despite life's occasional knocks. They decide not to be average, to wake up earlier, work harder, live life better and grow stronger. This is the mental attitude of champions.

When you decide to win no matter your emotional state or how difficult the circumstances, it gives you the power and capacity to take action. Some people would rather sleep all day than take massive action on their dreams. Some people would rather look for excuses than find out and do what it takes to make their dreams possible. Your words are not the proof of whether or not you are fully invested in your vision, your actions and total commitment are.

No matter the circumstances, someone is always making the most of it, doing something big and rising high despite their challenges. And if somebody else is, tell yourself, "It might as well be me!" If you want wealth, happiness and health, don't just become another talker; take massive action. That's the only way you will truly manifest your greatness.

The only way you are going to achieve extraordinary levels of success is if you take massive action. If you always wait for favourable conditions before you start working on your dreams you will never start. The best thing you can do for your dreams right now and that ultimate future you desire is not to simply just talk about it but to start. Super Athlete Wayde van Niekerk running for the gold and setting a New World Record didn't begin when he was competing at the pinnacle of his career at the Olympics, but it happened one day when he decided to start. Today I want to encourage you to be like Wayde van Niekerk and do not allow yourself to be distracted or discouraged by those who have never started. Keep your eyes firmly fixed on the prize and keep on running. And while you at it, remember...

100% of the opportunities you don't apply for will slip away,

100% of shots you don't take you miss,

100% of the competitions you don't enter you lose, start.

When you start, you open up the horizons for new opportunities and possibilities. Wayde van Niekerk didn't start out highly successful, but he started out as the underdog just like you perhaps that decided one day to run towards your dream. Resources might have been limited, the setting unfavourable and support poor for him, but nothing could stop his go.

He kept on diligently working on his dreams, fuelled by a burning conviction in his heart, a compelling obsession and total commitment to win. Each early morning practice session and each failed attempt was edging his way closer and closer to the prize until one day in front of a roaring crowd and millions of spectators from all around the world he not only won the Olympic Gold Medal but set a New World Record surpassing all his competitors. **His victory was no mere coincidence but symbolic of his will and total commitment to win.** Despite where you are now or the number of obstacles you have to overcome, whatever you do be like Wayde van Niekerk today; give your total commitment and don't stop.

BENEFITS OF EQUIPPING YOURSELF

Total commitment requires you to be at the forefront of improving yourself. It's important to equip yourself with everything necessary to experience the maximum benefit of your talent. A developed gift will propel you into extraordinary levels of success. It's been said that, *A bar of iron cost $5, made into horseshoes its worth $12, made into needles its worth $3500, made into balance springs for watches, it's worth is $300 000.* Your own value is also determined by what you are able to make of yourself. Never settle for less when you have the potential to be worth so much more.

BENEFITS OF EQUIPPING YOURSELF

- ✓ *Equipping yourself increases your chances of being hired*
- ✓ *It can exponentially increase your market value*
- ✓ *You will be seen as an authority*
- ✓ *You will be seen as reliable and respected amongst your peers*
- ✓ *You will receive lucrative financial incentives and be more likely to be immediately placed in senior roles*
- ✓ *You will possess superior knowledge that places you ahead of the competition*
- ✓ *You will produce high quality work second to none*

SUSTAIN THE MOMENTUM

*One of the common reasons people fall from
great to average is because they become complacent and
stop sustaining the momentum.*

Without total commitment to the dream people limit their success. Without sustaining the momentum people soon lose their drive, can easily become complacent and fall from glory. Look at the sad fall of the once dominant Nokia Mobile Company because of their inability to innovate fast enough and live by the cardinal rule of the 4th Component of Vision: Sustaining the Momentum. When you don't sustain the momentum you will pay a painful price.

People who stop moving become comfortable. When you become comfortable you stop learning. When you stop learning you stop growing, and where growth ceases innovation stops. No wonder people often like to relive former glory days through telling the same old stories of past achievements repeatedly. What they don't realize is that the best glory in life is in living life to its maximum output, from one victory to the next. That is the essence of sustaining the momentum. It's the realization that if I am still alive there is so much more for me to do. That I have achieved this significant milestone, that's wonderful, but what's next?!

Another downside of not sustaining the momentum is that when people encounter devastating failure they easily become disheartened and sadly give up on their big dreams altogether. When Steve Jobs got fired from the company he started instead of being paralyzed by such a disappointing blow he decided to start a new company and guess what he called it? "NEXT!" Your best life is not behind you but it's in front of you - keep moving. And if you encounter a wall, don't stop. If the world says "no!" you say, "next!" If they tell you it can't be done, say, "next!" And if your friends are winning celebrate with them because that means you're next!

POOR BEGINNINGS CAN BECOME POWERFUL ENDINGS

After being shot in the head at point blank range by the Taliban for her bold advocacy for girls to be educated, and miraculously surviving the traumatic experience, Malala Yousafzai became the youngest person to be awarded the Nobel Peace prize at the tender age of 25. Often our most painful moments lead to our greatest victories.

When things go terribly wrong and you experience the unfortunate devastation of life's occasional knocks like Malala, it often is surprising who you become in the process. Malala could never have imagined that her courage to stand up for what she believed would one day lead her to be awarded the Nobel Peace prize, write a bestselling memoir and become a renowned education activist around the world. Had she any choice in the matter she would have gladly skipped the pain and thereby miss out on destiny.

It was devastating what happened to her, but I can guarantee you if you would ask her if she would be willing to go through all that again if she knew what she would become in the process she would answer with an unequivocal yes! There is purpose to your pain. You might not always understand your process, but there is always a higher purpose.

Sadly, people often make the mistake of judging their poor beginning with someone's strong ending. Like Malala, your story might have only begun, but if you continue just a little further, lift your chin up, keep your head up, stay focused and keep on moving then maybe you will find you have produced that bestselling book you've always dreamed of, started that business or maybe even found your special someone. That's why you should never give up in the middle of your story. Your poor beginning might turn out to be a powerful ending.

> *In order to sustain the momentum you must be self-disciplined, pace yourself, be willing to adapt when necessary and stay hungry.*

SELF-DISCIPLINE

So what is self-discipline? It is defined in many instances as many things, namely: self-restraint, self-governance and strictness. A standard set by an individual or organization to be upheld. To be uncompromising in resolve, determined to stick to plans and laser focused in objective.

But what is self-discipline in its truest essence? To be self-disciplined means to be a disciple of a certain code and being a disciple means to be a follower, a devotee, to strictly adhere to orders, and obey and abandon all else but that cause. Like an athlete would strictly follow their training program to become the best they can be; like a student would study hard and thoroughly research their subject matter, even losing track of time, and like a salmon fish swimming upstream in a predator infested river to reach its destination. Ah yes, that's the spirit of self-discipline. Without a doubt, you cannot sustain the momentum and reach the summit of your dreams without this quality.

All super athletes are self-disciplined. Self-Discipline is an undeniable trait for greatness on all levels. Self-Discipline will create the boundaries that protect you and cultivate the routines that propel you. Your self-discipline is what will keep you going on the days when you are less motivated. If you lack self-discipline the vision gets neglected and your dream no matter how fervent in the beginning is eventually abandoned.

Self-discipline will enable you to follow through with the strict measures it requires to ensure your dreams become a reality. Self-discipline will heighten your awareness of time and how you choose to utilize it. Self-discipline reinforces high focus, because it will cause you to pay attention to the details and also help you to strategize and make clear cut decisions on your priorities. Self-discipline is very essential when reaching to accomplish one's dreams. The absence of self-discipline will lead to chaos and broken dreams.

PACE YOURSELF AGAINST YOURSELF

I was running one day and I often try my best to be in the lead pack. This day it was no different. I have been a runner all my life as a hobby I enjoy, but by far no super athlete like Usain Bolt. But the one principle I learnt in my running days was that if you stay with the lead pack long enough you can dramatically increase your chances of winning as you take on their philosophy and feed off their enthusiasm. On this particular day however, I quickly became exhausted and I realized that if I did not slow down, I could burn out and not even get the chance to complete the race. The problem was not that I was a bad runner, it was just that the other runners came prepared and I was not.

There are moments when you are running towards your dreams that it's better to slow down and pace yourself against yourself but benchmark yourself against the best because as long as you are still running it means you still have a chance to catch up. All top achievers didn't start at the top, they started at the bottom and worked their way up. Pace yourself against yourself but benchmark yourself against the best. You need to stay in tune with the seasonal demand upon your life so that you don't get burnt out in the process and can allocate resources adequately.

ADAPT PROMPTLY

One day I was selling tickets for one of my transformational seminars. Ticket sales were going poorly on the online platform and I didn't print tickets because I wanted to direct all ticket sales to the one online platform. However, when I discovered how slow ticket sales were online I immediately printed a fresh batch of tickets about two weeks before my seminar was scheduled and sold one ticket at a time by hand. It was an exhausting process but selling tickets by hand gave me far greater traction than my online ticket sales did. If I did not adapt fast enough my seminar would have been a complete failure. Feedback and evaluating the data is vital if you are to reposition yourself and increase your chances of winning.

If you never pause to evaluate your results, it may be the very reason you get overtaken by the competition and fail dismally. What if Nokia was more prompt in responding to the change in dynamics in the mobile field arena. Would they still have been the global leader today that they were in their heydays? In a world where disruption can happen as quickly as a mouse click, you either adapt promptly or experience devastating failure.

STAY HUNGRY

While you are sustaining the momentum it's important to remember that the key to staying ahead is to stay hungry. The reason why billionaires Richard Branson and Warren Buffet don't sit back and relax on an exotic beach all day is because they have learnt this important principle, that is, to stay hungry. Yesterday's success is not what keeps them excited. It's their potential to be more. No matter how good you are there is always a next level. If you are hungry it doesn't matter who is ahead of you, you can overtake them. Success comes to the hungriest and determined, not the most talented.

Arnold Schwarzenegger is a brilliant case study to look at for a lesson in sustaining the momentum. He went from being a highly successful body builder with an impressive five Mr. Universe and seven Mr. Olympia first price wins, to a top Hollywood action star and finally Governor of California. Those who sustain the momentum like Arnold Schwarzenegger rarely look forward to retiring; their obsession with being more is what constantly drives them to achieve even greater levels of success that evades others.

In order to sustain your current success and reach beyond you must be willing to push yourself further and multiply the amount of action you are willing to put in. When one goal is achieved that's not a signal to slow down but rather allows you to leverage off the momentum created to achieve more extraordinary levels of success.

There is so much potential that remains dormant in countless people for this simple reason - they easily settle and are not bold enough to sustain the momentum and multiply their results. That's the main reason the small corner shop in the community never moves beyond where it is to become a global enterprise like Walmart although it might have the same potential and have been operating for the same number of years. If you are not taking massive action on your dreams and continuing to push yourself further I can guarantee you that you are falling behind and limiting how far you can go.

Sustaining the momentum will form the habits of winning and ensure your victories are not short-lived. Every master was once an amateur that kept on moving. Every professional was once a beginner that kept on moving, and if you sustain the momentum that means you are next.

BENEFITS OF SUSTAINING THE MOMENTUM

✓ *Removes the limitations*

✓ *Breeds innovation*

✓ *Brings new challenges that gives you more opportunities to grow*

✓ *Causes you to think creatively*

✓ *Strengthens your impact*

✓ *Gives you new victories*

✓ *Exponentially increases your value*

EMBRACE FAILURE

*Mastery is not achieved by those who never failed, but
by those who refuse to be overcome by it.*

The idea of failure on the road to success is widely romanticized. The reality is failure is devastating to deal with, and when one fails hard, it often takes a while to get up again. The year I couldn't progress to the next grade in high school, I failed hard. The day I experienced total financial collapse while pursuing my dreams, I failed hard. The day I wanted to commit suicide, I failed hard. How hard have you failed perhaps? Everyone will go through times where they experience disappointing failure and things go terribly wrong, but I want to let you know that it's absolutely okay. It's not about how hard you fail but about how well you get back up again.

Every dream that has ever been turned into reality has experienced tremendous failures. Failures are actually stepping stones into greater achievements.

It's only through the furnace of failure that a remarkable character is produced that is able to gracefully withstand pressure and setbacks and go on to achieve extraordinary success. It takes courage, maturity and an iron will to get up again when you have failed. Any good team will tell you that there were many days where they had off days. The off days helped them appreciate the value of the win and play better. **Similarly, in your own life you will discover that every failure you went through was worth the lesson; it made you wiser, better and stronger.**

They say you learn more from a game you lose than a game you win. Sometimes the loss is to your advantage, it moves you backward temporarily in order to move you forward permanently. Failures can be a life changing experience and can represent a turning point for you that changes everything.

Jack Ma, founder of a multibillion E-commerce store Alibaba, was one of 24 people who applied to work at KFC when KFC first came into his town. 23 people were accepted; however, he was the only one to be rejected. Those who have achieved greatly are those who have often failed gravely. The 5th Component of Vision: Embracing Failure is about having the right perspective of failure as a necessary step in the success equation. How else would one then be able to measure success if you have never failed? **That's why every no, every closed door, every failure and every rejection is part of your journey. You will never truly appreciate the beauty of success if you've never experienced the bitterness of failure.**

PROTECT YOUR HEART

When you do fail, which anyone who steps out to pursue their dreams will eventually, it's important that you protect your heart. You will mess up and get disappointed even more but your reaction to what happens to you will determine whether you become bitter or better - choose the latter. Don't pursue any goals because you have a point to prove to somebody - do it with the pure motive that it's part of your life's purpose. Victory is indeed sweet, but don't allow yourself to be contaminated by the bitter waters you had to pass through on your way to the top.

STAY HUMBLE

Failure will help you stay humble. Leadership is not about being brilliant, it's about humility because brilliant leaders have fallen, and their roles have been forgotten. Talent is your ability, humility is for your longevity. In whatever you pursue, no matter how lofty the goal, it's important that you stay humble.

EMBRACE GRATITUDE

It's important to maintain a healthy perspective of where you are now in your life in relation to where you were whenever you experienced failure. Remember you used to pray for a better job and God gave you one? Remember you always wished you'd have a nice car and a fancy house and now you have them? Remember you used to pray for a life-partner and now you have one? Question is, did you get so used to and comfortable with what you have currently, that like so many you've lost sight of the boundless blessings of your beautiful sunshine trying to look for the pot of gold at the end of the rainbow?!

Don't lose the passion and zeal over what was once considered a miracle. Don't become so ungrateful that you forget the miracle of where God has taken you from. Although it is great to celebrate the big victories, it's equally important to celebrate the little ones from time to time as well. Every milestone is a miracle you made it to and is worth celebrating. Protect your heart, stay humble and remain grateful.

HAVING THE FULL PICTURE

A casino is structured in such a way that they have the statistical edge. They know with the information they have that it's only a matter of time till they come out on top. They therefore are willing to lose some, knowing that in the end they will gain even more.

You see they have the full picture. Having the full picture of how it's going to work out in the end gives them the strength to hold on, the power to persevere and the assurance that it's going to be okay. They are aware no matter how difficult circumstances may look or how much losses they incur, in the end the house always comes out on top and it's not over until they win. Just like the casino, in life you must be willing to take those losses gracefully, knowing that in the end things will work out in your favour because it's not over until you win.

Michael Jordan must have had the full picture; in his highly successful career in the NBA he missed 9000 shots. Don't be afraid to fail - take the shots. No matter how many shots you miss you can still be massively successful just like him.

LET THE RESULTS SPEAK FOR ITSELF!

Life is hard, and honestly, it's not going to get any easier. To win you must be willing to pay the price and make sacrifices repeatedly. Winning big is not going to come easy. It's a long shot to extraordinary levels of success and if you are not willing to fight for what you want you not going to make it. What do you do when your reality looks nothing like your dream? What do you do when you've given it your all and you still fall short and have nothing to show for it?

Can you imagine the ridicule and persecution Thomas Edison must have faced when attempting to invent the light bulb and having nothing but failure to show for his efforts? And the people's comments may have been: "come on now old Eddy you've been at it 500 times already, give it a rest man! You are embarrassing yourself. Why can't you just be like us normal people. I know what it is, you think you better than us!"

Yet he kept on moving forward and the 500th became the 600th attempt and people started speaking around town about him more fiercely saying, "hey there have you seen Eddy, yeah, he's at it again, talking to himself, busy with that lightbulb thingy, you know he's crazy right, haha!" It's hard to carry around the burden of a dream when nobody sees it but you. It's hard to go on when it feels like you in it alone.

And there were days where it looked like Edison was not going to make it, undoubtedly. There were times he wanted to give up unquestionably, but he had the will to win and kept on working on his dream day and night, step by step, one inch at a time. He had a big dream and was totally committed to the process. It seemed slow but he was making progress, it seemed he was taking too long but the distance between him and the dream became shorter and shorter each day, it was not over until he won.

He marched onward and forward until the 600th attempt became the 700th and 800th. I don't know about you, but this man failed a lot and if it was you and I we would probably have given up a long time ago. He religiously lived by the 5th Component of Vision and kept on moving forward. Then finally came the 999th attempt, until it became the 1000th attempt where he reached his breakthrough! Just like Thomas Edison, **you have to see it before everyone else sees it, believe it before everyone else believes it and keep on going even when you encounter countless failure.**

You might be asking yourself, "how long does one really have to work on their dreams?" My advice to you is to be like Thomas Edison - forget the crowd, forget the haters and naysayers, pay them no mind and do whatever it takes. Forget the timeline, just have faith that in the end it will work out and do it as long as it takes, until you silence your critics and the results speak for itself.

COMEBACK STRONG!

During my high school years I failed a grade. I was so disappointed and felt like such a loser who had brought shame to myself and my family and didn't understand why. It was only in my final year of high school when a group called, The 4Change Foundation, came to my school for the very first time. The 4Change Foundation's focus was on offering guidance and mentorship to troubled boys, like I was during those days. Going through their program redirected my focus, and gave me a new sense of mission and purpose. It was my divine appointment, my turning point. Had I never failed in high school and matriculated a year earlier I would have missed them.

Sometimes God will deliberately hold you back from entering certain seasons not because He's forgotten about you, but because He is still busy forming you. It's easy to get despondent and feel like such a total loser during this time but could it perhaps be that that promotion you didn't get, that opportunity you might have missed was intentional and part of God's plan for your life?

Before an arrow is shot it must be pulled back first and the more it is pulled back the further it will go. Might it perhaps be that you are just in the pulling phase and the reason why you have not achieved certain things sooner is because you are still being stretched. Your destiny is so much greater, and God allowed things to fall apart so that it could mould you to come back stronger?

Back then I could never foresee that my failure was part of God's plan and I would one day become a sought after speaker and author of multiple books. If you have failed numerous times and find yourself at a painful place I want to encourage you today - don't give up! The stretching of the arrow is purposeful, the final chapters of your story has not been written yet and you can comeback stronger.

OH NO!

When I broke up with the girl that was somewhat the catalyst for my first book I was devastated. I had dated many girls before her, and was fooling around, and just when I changed my ways and decided to fully commit the relationship, believing I would get married to that girl it abruptly ended. I was heartbroken and had an, "Oh no, not this again" experience. Have you ever had an, "Oh no, not this again?!"

The Oh no experiences hits you in the gut, keeps you up into the wee hours of the morning and can torment your soul. Another break-up, "Oh no, not this again!"

Another disappointment, Oh no...

Another failure, Oh no...

Another job that didn't work out, Oh no...

Another setback, Oh no...

"I have been through this before, how can I go through something like this again" you wonder...

And suddenly flash backs of how it made you feel back then, the disappointment, the hurt, and the betrayal is replayed in your mind as if it's on a repeated loop. And you feel like this time you just had enough, you might not pull through, that you've reached your breaking point, and about to go off the edge of the cliff. Sometimes the Oh no is God's way of telling you that you have not learnt the lesson yet to grow in order to advance to the next phase.

I want you to realize that it is okay to fail from time to time. It's okay that there will be days where you feel like lying in bed all day, less excited about your dream and just feel like doing absolutely nothing. It's okay to sometimes not be okay and realize that it's still okay. The Oh no failures will humble you and often **some of your most important lessons will come from painful and bitter places.** And when you perhaps just see it from another angle, perhaps the Oh no's is a blessing dressed up in disguise when things have worked out and you begin to look back.

Thomas Edison just needed one success while creating the light bulb and it was enough to make up for all his previous failures. Once you finally achieve the splendour of your dreams it will make up for all the Oh no experiences and the hell you've been through. There's a lesson in every misfortune. So, if you are failing - keep on going. You can lose many battles, but don't lose the war. The current obstacles are laying the foundation of your future success. In you resides the seeds of greatness, and it's not over until you win.

JUST BE STRONG

While confiding in one of my friends about the troubled season I had been through and how there were many days I just wanted to give up, she listened to me attentively. Later that day she bought me a cold drink and a Cadbury P.S Chocolate, and on it was written a simple but encouraging message, "Just Be Strong!" And that's what I want to end the 5th Component of Vision with.

Just be strong when your heart is broken, your knees are buckled and your head is clouded because it's filled with pain so intense you can't explain. Just be strong while battling with unresolved issues and wishing somehow you could go back in time to change things, and avoid the feeling of finding yourself at such a disappointing low.

Just be strong in the midst your tribulation. It's clear that when you are in pursuit of the prize your commitment to it will be met with heavy opposition and countless challenges. The terrain is certainly dangerous, and the challenges are complex but don't act surprised. With a dream as big as yours would you expect any less? Just stay strong.

The day, I found myself in hospital after experiencing a devastating failure and mental breakdown. An Oh no experience that placed me under psychological evaluation as I seriously contemplated suicide. One of the fellow patients asked me a personal question, he said, "you seem so wise, why are you here with us?!" It's like a pin dropped... His question caught me completely off-guard. I paused and thought deeply before I could respond and then finally said, "Butterflies can't become butterflies without the process, diamonds can't become diamonds without the process, gold can't become gold without the process and even champions get knocked down from time to time and experience breaking point. You are who you are today not because it was easy, but because you made it through your process. Just be strong."

It was Ron Kenoly who said, "If you catch fire don't hold it, if you go through hell don't stop". In other words, he was saying, just be strong, it's not over until you win. Just be strong because somebody is counting on you to make it, for you to stand up and pull through so that you will be there to catch them when they fall.

Just be strong although you embarrassed yourself. Wear it as a proud scar in remembrance of where you were and what you had to make it through. **Some failures protect you against future knocks, so that when you look at it in hindsight you will actually wish you failed sooner, so that you might have learnt the lesson quicker.** Just be strong.

Just be strong. Although those lessons were very painful, it made you stronger and prepared you for the better.

You don't have any idea how powerful and immensely gifted you are until certain things push you into that direction. And I am not going to pretend with you and even say that the hurt, the failure and what you went through was easy, but God knew that that last push was just what you needed to push you off the cliff not so that you would fall, but to push you into your destiny so that you can finally discover your wings and soar. Just be strong.

BENEFITS OF FAILURE

- ✓ *Failure helps you appreciate the value of winning*

- ✓ *Failure increases your capacity to handle painful dispointment and when things go terribly wrong*

- ✓ *Failure keeps you humble and grounded*

- ✓ *Failure will cause you to break bad habits that might hamper your success*

- ✓ *Failure challenges you to explore new strategies for uncommon success*

- ✓ *Failure makes you more susceptible to creativity and innovation*

- ✓ *Failure better prepares you for a life of extraordinary results*

- ✓ *Failure gives you the courage to finally take the necessary actions towards pursuing your dreams no matter how great the risk*

HIGH FOCUS

*The primary reasons why people and organizations fail
is because of broken focus.*

In a world where we are bombarded daily with vast distractions, the ability to stay highly focused is an undeniable trait to possess for those who hope to achieve outstanding success. The 6th Component of Vision, High Focus, is about developing the discipline to stay away from the tasks that do not fall within the area of your primary focus, and maximizing your time on those core activities that are central to your life's purpose. That's why; sometimes saying no without explaining yourself is part of your focus.

I am foolish at a lot of things but I am great in the area of my primary focus. A lot of people feel pressured to perform in areas they are not suited for unaware that when they do it diminishes their chances of success.

Just because something is exciting or trending doesn't necessarily mean it's what you should be doing. One of life's greatest tragedies is that countless people are trying to be successful in areas that they have not been gifted to perform. **What made Bill Gates a billionaire was not his search for a big pay day but his obsession in delivering massive value in the area of his core focus.** When you focus on the areas you are suited for your chances of success are much higher, because you are likely to possess superior knowledge and a rare skill level.

The strong eyesight of an eagle enables it to have the high focus necessary to spot prey from miles away. To successfully capture its prey the eagle will narrow its focus, and remain firm enough so that no obstacle serves as a deterrent until it has successfully seized its prey. An eagle doesn't just go for their prey but they must bring themselves to a laser focus. Often people's clarity of vision is hindered by their inability to stay focused. How firm is your focus? Have a firm enough focus and the goal that your eyes are fixed on will soon be within your grasp.

The difference between someone having a PhD and someone having several different degrees that are unrelated to each other is focus. It's better to specialize in one discipline than to be wildly knowledgeable on many different ones. High focus gives you a winning edge and the best competitive advantage.

At the heart of mastery is focus. A gun shot with a telescopic site is more effective and gives you greater accuracy than a shot gun because of its focus. If you are hungry, and there is a group of wildebeest in a jungle, if you aim everywhere you might miss them all. But if you aim at just one, you might hit one although the others might get away. **Focus on the few important things you do exceptionally well and ignore the rest.**

Nobody goes to a heart surgeon for a dental job, nor to a dentist for heart surgery. The reason is because although each one is a specialist; their focus is different. People choose you because of your focus. Your high focus becomes the compelling reason they would like to work with you. **That's why your focus is more important than your intelligence. Your focus is what distinguishes you from the crowd.**

FINDING YOUR FOCUS

When two of the richest man in the world, Warren Buffet and Bill Gates was asked by Bill's dad to write down on a piece of paper the one thing that determined their success the most, both wrote down, "focus". The most important thing you will ever need to discover in your life is the area of your primary focus. It's not how much money you desire to get paid, because how much you get paid is the by-product of delivering massive value in the area of your primary focus and not the main goal.

Finding your focus is similar to what we have discussed in the 1st Component of Vision, about purpose. Your focus is the area that speaks to your why; your life's work. There are areas in your life where you are profoundly gifted and there are areas you are not. That is why it is so important to seek out the competence of those who possess the expertise in areas you are not gifted in. Because when the task exceeds your level of skill it is necessary for you to delegate it. **Trying to do something that you are not suited for is a misuse of your time and mismanagement of your life.** That's why I would advise against going where you cannot perform well. You cannot lead everywhere, trying to do so will only make you less effective.

An Eagle not in flight and hanging around chickens its whole life might grow up thinking it's like its fellow chickens and destined to be there, but put it in the sky and its genius emerges. Unlike the Eagle, the reason why most people fail to tap into their brilliance is because they haven't found the area of their primary focus. Your focus is your difference and the only area you've been divinely qualified and uniquely equipped to dominate. **Never move away from the primary purpose of why you exist. Broken focus is not just costly but detrimental.**

When I didn't know my focus I tried out different ventures and ideas that promised big gains and failed dismally. On the road towards finding your focus, you are going to fail at multiple things and that's okay, the failure is not a final reflection of your full potential, it just helps redirect you towards what truly matters to you and discover your sweet spot.

The reason why J.K Rolling, author of the renowned Harry Potter series could finally focus on the one area that truly mattered to her the most - her writing, was because she encountered great failure and this caused her to focus. And what was the result of her focus? Worldwide success, and prominence.

You will not achieve noteworthy success in any area of life until you've found your focus. If you can fail in areas you are not gifted in nor love, might as well give it your all pursuing what you love instead. Build on your strengths and not weaknesses. Your focus must lead you closer and not further away from your dreams. Finding your focus is discovering the primary area that will become your life's work. For J.K Rolling it was writing novels and for celebrated mega TV host Oprah Winfrey it was being a talk show host. Their brilliance is in their focus. They devoted their time and energy to one dream over a considerable period of time that yielded them outstanding results. The key to getting further with less is focus. **Before you can produce above average results you need to become highly focused.**

In the movie Kungfu Panda 3, the hero, Panda, is promoted and becomes the master over the rest of the five dragon warriors. At the beginning of his new leadership role he fails dismally. He later has an epiphany where he discovers that the key to unlocking the hidden greatness of the dragon warriors is to focus on their known strengths and not their weaknesses.

The outcome, they finally became the exceptional dragon warriors they were destined to be.

What is hindering you from tapping into your inner mastery? Doubt, distractions or fear perhaps? By not living life from the area of your primary focus is the greatest disservice you can do to yourself and humanity. Focus on those core activities that bring you the greatest value and where you can make the biggest impact. And like Panda discovered, the rewards of living life from your primary focus far outweighs the losses of making the shift today.

GROWTH THROUGH HIGH FOCUS

One of the keys to living a fulfilled life is to discover the gifts you are blessed with and area you would like to impact. That's why you should never seek growth without focus. More important than growth is how you grow.

The greatest area you should seek growth in is the area of your primary focus. If you love painting, study the greatest painters and adopt their ways, if it is music, do likewise. When you are highly focused you will evaluate everything you do in life whether it strengthens or diminishes that focus. That's why every book you read, every course you take or podcast you listen to must be in alignment with your primary focus and empower you for the life of your dreams.

Many seek to study a certain discipline because they are either pressured by their parents or because of lucrative financial incentives. Approached in that manner might bring short term victory but lack of fulfilment in the long run. This is one of the most common reasons many people are in great jobs that might pay well but it does not fulfil them because it's not central to their focus.

You should rather discover what you truly passionate about and equip yourself with everything necessary in order to experience the maximum benefit of that talent. And if studying a certain discipline is one of the requirements then your high focus will clearly define it.

BEING HIGHLY FOCUSED ENABLES YOU TO WORK SMART NOT HARD

Doing trivial things delays you from doing those core activities that are critical to your primary focus. Being excessively busy doesn't mean that you are more productive. The goal of any activity in regards to your high focus is to aim for the shortest path towards maximizing your results. Whether that entails defying the norms or working out a system to achieve your goal faster, if everyone is spending 10 000 hours, you can be the exception. Most pro ballet dancers start as early as the age of 5, since it takes years to develop the flexibility and technique in order to be a successful ballerina, yet Misty Copeland only started ballet at the age of 13, and went on to become a principal ballerina at the American Ballet Theatre despite the late start.

Just like Misty Copeland, don't allow society's norms to define whether or not you can achieve your goal in less time. There is no substitute for hard work, but if hard work is not done efficiently you could be wasting valuable time that could have been spent doing other meaningful activities. By all means work insanely hard, but do it in a smart way that doesn't consume your whole life so that you can pause to relish the moments with your loved ones and create special memories that will last a lifetime.

THREATS TO YOUR HIGH FOCUS

PAYING ATTENTION TO THE CRITICS

Paying attention to critics is an unnecessary distraction to fulfilling your dream. The cheetah is able to run so fast because of its ability to stay highly focused. Those who are highly focused are too preoccupied dominating in the area of their primary focus that they don't have time to waste on anything that is not serving that goal.

Moreover, if they didn't believe you when you started and if they don't believe you by now, it shouldn't surprise you, but know that if you can make it up to here, have the faith that you can make it all the way.

LACK OF A CLEAR FOCUS

In the absence of a clear focus menial activities consume your time and disorder becomes normal. When disorder becomes normal you are more prone to be affected and influenced by other people's ideas and opinions of what you should be.

TRYING TO PLEASE EVERYONE ELSE

Don't become so busy trying to please everyone else that you become the most neglected person. Stop borrowing yourself out like a library book. When you are constantly preoccupied with numerous activities not beneficial to your dream, it will be difficult for you to focus on the core objectives you wish to achieve.

In an airplane you are instructed by the Air Hostess to put on your oxygen mask first, and then when yours is firmly secured, you can help someone else. Sadly, too often, countless people are suffocating in difficult circumstances trying to please other people while they have not even put the mask on their own mouth first.

It's time for you to put on your mask and focus on what's highly important to you, because in a few years from now you will either say, "it wasn't easy, but it was worth it" or you will say "if only I worked harder, if only I was more focused..." Moreover, it's better to generously help others when you are in an empowered position.

FAILURE TO PRIORITIZE

Failure to prioritize is another major reasons people cannot focus, underperform and produce mediocre results. Many people would rather prioritize leisure than their dreams because it simply is not important enough. But when you understand the importance of your dream it will fill you with a burning obsession to fulfil it.

I financed my first and second book. It was my dream after all and not others', therefore I had to meet the bill. When your dream truly becomes important to you making time for it becomes the only option. You must be the first one to prioritize and finance your dreams. If you are not prepared to finance your dreams then you don't want it badly enough.

For some people it's not that they are too busy, it's just that they have their priorities wrong and are too preoccupied wasting their precious time and energy on activities that doesn't add any lasting value or take them further towards achieving their dreams. If it's not taking you further, making you better, or improving your results you should not be spending time on it. Being highly focused will allow you to block out unnecessary distractions and eliminate anything that is not serving your goals.

GREAT FORTUNES FOLLOW THE HIGHLY FOCUSED

The highly successful don't spread themselves too thin, nor do they fill their lives by being constantly busy with the wrong activities. A life of high focus is a simplified life in a complex world, as you can easily minimize distractions, prioritize your goals and determine the activities that are essential to your dream.

When Steve Jobs returned to the failing Apple in 1998, he decreased the product range from a vast 350 products to a lean 10 products. By refocusing on fewer products they could become more efficient and effective. A narrow product range boosted sales, increased their market share and allowed them to become unchallenged. **Many successful companies are what they are because of their ability to focus on delivering value in what they do best, consistently**. Great fortune awaits the highly focused.

Thomas Edison didn't just fail his way to success; he was so firm in his resolve to highly focus on achieving the set objective of perfecting the light bulb that he would not stop until it yielded him the exact results he was looking for. Founder of Tesla Motors, Elon Musk took his 180 million-dollar proceeds from PayPal and re-invested it into his dreams to the extent that he had to borrow money for rent. The thoughts of some people back then must have been, "why that's quite foolish!" I'd say he was only highly focused. If you are never willing to risk it all for what you love, then it means you don't want it badly enough. **Sometimes you have to give up, to go up and often you'll have to endure the humiliation of looking foolish and misunderstood for the sake of your dreams**

During the early stages of mega star comedian Kevin Hart's career he was a successful shoe salesman who was offered a lucrative new job opportunity with Nike. However, he enthusiastically declined the offer. Now, why would he do that you might ask? I'd say he found his focus. Have you found your focus? When you find your focus the difficult choices become easy and even the most lucrative opportunities that might distract you will become less desirable. Today Kevin Heart is not only one of Nike's brand ambassadors but one of the top personalities in comedy and one of the highest paid comedians in history. His focus produced far greater results than working for Nike could perhaps have ever done. Similarly, follow your focus and great fortunes will follow you.

MISFORTUNES OF LACK OF HIGH FOCUS

- ✓ *Lack of focus results in derailed dreams and is the catalyst of great failure.*

- ✓ *A mind without a focus is a hazard to itself*

- ✓ *Lack of focus will result in minimal progress and wasted time and resources*

- ✓ *Lack of focus results in giving up too soon. Most people don't focus on anything long enough to reap significant results or master it. The truly great causes require a lot of time and effort to reap significant results.*

- ✓ *Lack of focus hinders one's critical and logical thinking about the dream.*

- ✓ *Lack of focus will cause you to miss the detail and hinder you from giving your dream the maximum effort it demands.*

- ✓ *Lack of focus is the cause of mediocrity, since you won't be at a peak state to produce high quality work.*

- ✓ *Lack of focus is a trait of the disorganized. The unfocused like to multitask and may succeed in doing many tasks, but poorly.*

- ✓ *Lack of focus is a deterrent to greatness*

BENEFITS OF BEING HIGHLY FOCUSED

✓ *High focus is the starting point for great fortunes and manifestation of your dreams.*

✓ *High focus increases efficiency and improves productivity.*

✓ *When you are highly focused you don't need constant validation from external sources.*

✓ *When you are highly focused you become absolutely clear about what you want and can easily minimize distractions*

✓ *High focus produces brilliance*

✓ *The number one rule for high focus is not to diversify. Stick with what you know until you dominate.*

✓ *High focus gives you an unparalleled advantage*

✓ *High focus forms consistent habits that breed phenomenal results*

POWERFUL PARTNERSHIPS

*The quality of your life is a direct reflection of
the quality of your relationships.*

The 7th Component of Vision, Powerful Partnerships is arguably the most important component of vision. When you have made considerable progress with your dream you will notice how people in the form of partnerships will be attracted to you.

All your goals in life will either be enhanced or diminished by the quality of your relationships. No one gets very far in life alone. **Greatness never happens in isolation but is always a result of collaboration. The fool thinks he needs no one and often goes nowhere slowly.** Wise is he who establishes powerful partnerships before pursuing meaningful projects, for the success of any project undertaken is not always determined by the size of the dream, but the strength of the team.

In the movie *42*, Chadwick Boseman, played the role of Jackie Robinson who was best known for becoming the first black Major League Baseball player. He was being driven by a reporter, and he remarked to the reporter, "I don't like needing anybody". In turn the reporter responded by asking sarcastically, "is it okay if I keep driving you or should I just let you get out and walk?" I am sure that day Jackie Robinson was reminded about the value of partnership and realized that it could take him places his talent could not.

Not all partnerships are beneficial, the right partnerships are, know the difference. Those whose goals are lofty understand that having big dreams necessitates that they connect and build around them a strong team. They establish strategic partnerships that will be able to benefit the dream greatly and improve them significantly. That's why companies would gladly spend millions dollars for super athletes or celebrities to be their brand ambassadors as they are aware that if their brand is associated with the highly successful it raises not only the perception of their brand's value in the eyes of their customers but could also mean more profitability. You can only go as far, and rise as high as your partnerships do. The right partnership can give you more opportunities to grow and increase exponentially.

CUT YOUR LOSSES

A fascinating story comes to mind that I heard a while back about the Japanese Koi fish. It was noted that when you place the Koi fish in a small fish tank it usually grows to no more than five to seven centimeters but when placed in a lake it grows three times that size. You can never live out your lake potential when stuck in a fish bowl environment. You cannot achieve great things in the midst of mediocrity.

You only as strong as the people you decide to surround yourself with. You are only as effective as your relationships. Your potential will either be limited or enhanced based on the company you keep. Bad company corrupts good character no matter how noble the intent or lofty the ambition. Like the Koi fish, don't let anybody fool you by telling you that your environment or the people you hang out with regularly doesn't matter. **When you are exposed to certain environments the ratio of you making it can go considerably down or up. That's why the further you move away from some people the happier you are and the better life becomes.**

I am sure if you could look at your life right now you would notice how often you don't have the same friends you had 5 or 15 years ago, right? I've personally discovered this in my own endeavors. Partnerships often come and go like the wind. And that often doesn't mean that they are real bad people, it could simply mean that their part in your story is up.

Be willing to cut your losses and walk away from any places or people that's no longer serving or supporting your goals. If they are disturbing your spirit and are not good for your emotional health, let them go. Don't become too emotional or too attached. You must make peace with the fact that not everyone you start the journey with will end it with you. Forge bonds where it matters, cut your losses when it's toxic, and move on gracefully.

THE KEY TO FORMING PARTNERSHIPS

The key to forming powerful partnerships is your ability to judge who is better suited to further your goals. Friends might offer good emotional and moral support, but a strategic partnership will provide the skill and added horsepower to further worthwhile goals.

Additionally, not everyone that is not on your team is an opponent. Steve Jobs after he was reinstated as Apple's CEO in a bold move phoned Apple's chief rival Bill Gates of Microsoft to discuss how they could amicably settle their court case and how they could partner. In return Bill Gates injected millions in non-competing shares that helped drastically raise Apple's stock price and revive their former glory. If it's causing you more harm, it would be worthwhile to at times bury the hatchet with an enemy and form a partnership that will be mutually beneficial.

The shallow and insecure view everyone who is not in their corner as a looming threat. The secure understand that the stage is big enough for everyone to shine. They are more than willing to establish partnerships with others, and possibly like Steve Jobs, unlikely allies that will help them achieve their goals.

SOMEDAY PEOPLE

Don't share your big dreams with small minded and short-sighted people. Surround yourself with other dreamers and winners. People who are going somewhere in life, people who are action orientated and not just big talkers. And by all means, stay away from "Someday People". Maybe you know some of you them.

Someday people are irritating

Someday people are mediocre minds

Someday people do not live by a code of excellence

Someday people love to delay

Someday people are expert critics but professional nobodies

Someday people will talk about someone else's grass and fail to water their own

Someday people bring average results

Someday people are consumers and not contributors

Someday people's attitudes stink

Someday people never effect any positive change

Someday people are a cancer in society

Someday people are whiners not winners

Whatever you do, do yourself a favor, don't just stay away, but run from someday people!

IT'S A TEAM EFFORT

A common question people often ask about success is, "is it the team or the leadership that determines the success one reaches in life?" My answer is simple, both. It's a team effort. One cannot exist without the other. A gifted visionary needs an equally gifted team who will successfully execute the vision.

In the military a commander is recognized for a great military conquest, though at times he never even fought the battle, fired a weapon, or was the foot soldier in the cold, muddy trenches. Even the spaceflight Apollo 11 was not put on the moon by one man alone, it was a group effort.

The 7-time Formula 1 world champion racer, Michael Schumacher, wins the prize and takes the overall glory, but achieving his dreams was as much a team effort as it was individual effort. He wouldn't have won his races without his phenomenal pit team. He wouldn't have won his races without his amazing car. He wouldn't have won his races without the great technicians and doctors who were there to guide him every step of the way. Great was the dream, much was achieved, but he wouldn't have won it all without his world class team backing him.

Don't despise team effort, don't take all the glory for yourself, take time in thanking, appreciating and at times mentioning by name those key individuals who helped you win and achieve your dreams.

In 2008 after an unsuccessful season Coach Carlos Alberto Parreira resigned from coaching the South African national soccer team. He was the Brazilian coach who lead the Brazilian soccer team to victory in the 1994 FIFA World Cup. Why didn't he produce similar results for the South African team? The truth, the South African team was by far not the Brazilian team. There was a myriad of factors that contributed to Brazil being who they were as a world class soccer team. It was not solely based on the brilliant leadership of coach Parreira. When you remove the circumstances and the combination of those factors the results are not often as easily duplicated.

Undoubtedly coach Parreira didn't wait for a better team, he simply served his best at all stages, whether it was with Brazil or South Africa. Moreover his impact with Brazil is what opened more doors of opportunity and the reason he was selected in the first place to become the coach that would hopefully turn things around for the South African team. It's just that with the South African team there was a different set of variables at play that affected his overall results with the team.

Similarly, in your own life, the total effect of the 7 Components of Vision can only be seen when you use them all together. Success is not solely hinged on one factor. If that was the case many leaders wouldn't need anyone. But it's the contributing force of a combination of efforts. The books you read, the partnerships you form, your environment, your self-image, your total commitment, your determination, your ability to live by the right set of principles, your high focus and daily routines all contribute to your overall results. It takes team effort.

THE 3 PILLARS OF PARTNERSHIP

There are 3 Pillars of Partnership that I do encourage one to actively establish and grow in. Pillars because pillars are usually on the same level supporting the same structure. That is a useful reminder to be aware that each one has a unique role to play. However, the measure of each one's contribution will be different and must be respected.

1ST PILLAR: MENTORS

The first pillar is mentors. The shortest distance between outstanding success is to get the right mentor. Never take advice from those who bear no good fruit. Would you send your kid for piano lessons to a chef or somebody that is actually a professional pianist? Likewise, **model the proven, follow the successful.** Why, because they already have results in the area you looking to get results in. Success leaves a worn out path for you to follow in their footsteps.

Mentors are credible people that have a proven track record of high success in the areas you desire to grow and strategic partnerships that will stretch you. Learning from them is of surpassing and significantly improve your results.

Two common reasons people don't succeed; lack of immersion and no accountability. Immersion requires total commitment. Accountability requires a mentor; a mentor will help hold you accountable to the results you want. It's no coincidence that world-class teams all have coaches; it's a sign that they are intentional about their growth and the results they want. A mentor is one of the number one reasons some people are further and seem to reach their goals faster. A mentor will help you reach your goals faster and make sure that the risk you take is in line with your strategic goals.

Who are the mentors in your life who can be brutally honest with you and able to correct you without you taking offense? You will never change where you are going until you change who you are following. Your response to your mentor will determine how fast you grow. **Friends may give you emotional and moral support in times of trouble**

but a mentor will provide you with excellent leadership and direction for your life. They are the sober counsel you draw from, able to stretch your vision and increase your competence. You don't need many mentors in order to improve your result, but the right mentor will empower you to experience exponential growth.

2ND PILLAR: PEERS

Your peers are the people on the same level as you. They have the same agenda, can add substantial value to your dream and you are likely to have great synergy. Bill Gates and Paul Allen, founders of Microsoft, and also childhood friends, were obsessed with computers, and had a passion for entrepreneurship. This made their partnership such a major success.[1] With powerful partnerships you can leverage off the skills and expertise of others.

You can't do all things well so who you partner with is very important. Moreover, you cannot build effectively with everyone. It is better to work on a few meaningful relationships than to be widely popular without solid relationships. The 6th Component of Vision, High Focus, is not often talked about in relation to quality relationships, but you cannot build any meaningful relationship without it. And how you treat one relationship that you often take for granted will determine how you treat others. How you manage the few relationships will empower you with the skills to better handle the masses.

BUILD WITH A FOCUSED TEAM

When you are focused you not too bothered about who abandons your vision, because your focus is on A players, not A quitters. The wrong team can never steer a company forward no matter how good the strategy. The right people can always take a company forward no matter how bad the economy. It's not about improving the quality of the process, it's about getting quality people. The old saying *"you are only as strong as your weakest link"* holds true.

The wrong people are more painful than a sprained ankle. They have poor habits, zap your energy and hamper your results. The right people are team players, people you can readily rely on and offer support in tough times. They are self-driven and motivated; they produce results not hamper it. They are focused on performance not processes. A focused team can drastically shift the culture of an organization.

It's not about the quantity of people you have on your team but it's about the quality of people. The fewer the people, the deeper the bond. Ensure that you have a small inner circle that you can trust, are loyal and will not easily break their allegiance with you when it seems beneficial to them.

3RD PILLAR: MENTEES

Leaders that do not empower those following in their footsteps are not just insecure, but risk having what they have built totally collapsing. As you realize each goal, there will be times where you are blessed with the resources and the wisdom to give back by mentoring those following in your footsteps.

At some stage in your life it should be your greatest joy to resign the reigns and pass the baton. Equip those who you will pass the baton to. You don't have to be intimidated by those rising successes when you can be part of it. Nelson Mandela retired gracefully at the pinnacle of his career. He placed the welfare of the people above his desire for power. Despite his passing his legacy continues to live on with even greater vigor.

In all these 3 pillars of partnership it is valuable to know that any partnership you form is always a privilege granted and not a right demanded. Understanding the tenets of each partnership avoids a lot of misunderstandings and unnecessary conflict from occurring. And maintaining a code of reciprocity ensures these partnerships are not short-lived.

THE WAY OF THE GEESE

Have you ever wondered why Geese fly in a V-shaped formation? Well, the fact is, they have realized that by flying together in this manner the formation creates lift in power, increases their speed, and the overall rate of reaching their destination by 70.1 %.

The ones following behind the leading pack experience less turbulence, exert less effort and thus they are more effective and efficient. As a result, they are able to conserve energy, travel much further and reach their destination quicker. Clearly, there are vast advantages available in partnerships.

Nothing great has ever been achieved alone. Two heads are better than one, in much the same way that many hands make the work lighter. We do better and achieve more together. True lasting greatness only happens in partnerships.

The 7 Components of Vision forms part of your strategic partnerships and by applying these 7 Components of Vision you possess the proven formula for extraordinary success. There are however no short cuts to success and often the bigger the dream the longer it takes. But when you get knocked down repeatedly and don't become disheartened, have the audacity to believe in the nobility of your dream and courage to continue then it will only be a matter of time until your ultimate dreams have fully materialized.

BENEFITS OF HAVING MENTORS

- ✓ *All top athletes have mentors, you cannot be a winning team without one*

- ✓ *A mentor will help you stay focused and perform at optimum*

- ✓ *They will help you think and do things differently*

- ✓ *They can help you cut through the years that comes from learning the hard way*

- ✓ *Their wisdom and experience gives you a competitive advantage*

- ✓ *They provide valuable insight and excellent leadership*

- ✓ *They bring out the best in you*

- ✓ *They have figured out the formula to success*

- ✓ *They can help you benefit from the process without the pain*

FROM THE AUTHOR

Thank you for reading The 7 Components of Vision. If you enjoyed this book (or even if you didn't) please visit amazon or kindle books, and be so kind to write a brief review. You are also more than welcome to send your review to info@ elroyrcook.com

Your feedback is important to me and will help other readers decide whether to read the book too.

If you'd like to get notifications of new releases and special offers on my books, please join my email list by sending an email to the same email already provided.

Wishing all the best!

El-Roy

ENDNOTES

1   http://www.businessinsider.com/10-super-successful-co-founders-and-why-their-partnerships-worked-2010-7?op=1

Tim Barton, *"How Many People Are Financially Independent During Retirement?"* (News, Retirement Planning: 30 May 2012) http://retire.areavoices.com/2012/05/30/how-many-people-are-financially-independent-during-retirement/ *19 November 2014*

Carole Cadwalladr, *"Nora Roberts: The woman who rewrote the rules of romantic fiction"* (Romance TheObserver 20 November 2011) Gaurdian News

http://www.theguardian.com/books/2011/nov/20/nora-roberts-interview-romance-fiction *11 July 2014*

Inside The Games, *"Elite Athletes Spend 10000 Hours Training For The London 201e"* (18 November 2010) http://m.insidethegames.biz/olympics/summer-olympics/2012/11108-elite-athletes-spend-10000-hours-training-for-london-2012 *10 July 2014*

Richard Edwards, *"Pride of Sport Awards: Teen swimming sensation Jessica Fullalove 'inspired' by Michael Phelps"* (Sport, 08 October 2014) http://www.mirror.co.uk/sport/pride-sport-awards-teen-swimming-4402719 *11 July 2014* Source - Mirror online

http://www.businessinsider.com/10-super-successful-co-founders-and-why-their-partnerships-worked-2010-7?op=1

www.ingramcontent.com/pod-product-compliance
Lightning Source LLC
Chambersburg PA
CBHW050954050726
47592CB00007B/2572